Acknowledgement

This book is dedicated to the blessings I have enjoyed
being the product of a hard working father and mother,
Solomon and Marthell Le Flore from which I inherited a
legacy of truth, fairness, hard work and most importantly
love.
It is also in recognition of the blessings of a wonderful
wife, Angela, and four wonderful daughters, Melanie,
Noelle, Natalie, and Nadia.
A special thanks to Angela, Nadia, and Natalie who served
as critics, editors, and inspirational support for this project.
Above all, I want to thank God who shares a common
place inside all of the people mentioned above.

Table of Contents

Introduction

It is virtually impossible to make progress in your life without a solid foundation. Indeed, it is a solid foundation that forms a basis of your understanding. Without understanding, you will have trouble trying to navigate the waters that constitute your economic life.

Have you ever felt as though you had a lot more to offer this world than what you are currently giving? Have you ever felt as though you had the potential for more but there were forces holding you back? You are not alone. The March 16, 2014 article in USA Today, entitled, "Slow Start, Shaky Future for Millennials", foretells of the woes of an economically constrained generation. Millennials are those people that reach adulthood on or after the year 2000. While this generation has experienced the effects of an increased cost of living, Millennials are not the only generation living an economically constrained life. In fact, the majority of people live economically constrained lives. But what does an economically constrained life actually entail? Well, an economically constrained life is a life consisting of multiple lost opportunities.

Lives are often constrained because opportunities have been hijacked by some other interest. In most situations, the constraints are due to waste and excess, which are both caused by corporate-driven interests. Control of resources is a money driven activity practiced by many corporations. These corporate interests seek to control, through money, access to resources needed for human survival.

There is nothing more debilitating to a young person's life then to not be able to provide for themselves. Many of the social ills that affect our society stem from people not being able to provide for themselves. I was once told that people do things for one of two reasons: either inspiration or desperation. Hopefully, this book will inspire you to change your thinking about your economic possibilities and allow you to work to alleviate your economic constraints by becoming a member of the Gift Economic Community.

There is substantial evidence that those systems and institutions that were formally put in place to help further society have failed the majority of people. In particular, the facts associated with the higher education system in the US are pretty dismal. According to CBS News and NerdWallet, over half of the doctors produced by US medical schools say that if they had it to do over again they would choose another profession. As disheartening as this sounds, it comes with good reason, due to the length of study, cost of education, and ultimately, the working conditions.

The disappointment with the U.S. higher education system does not stop with medical professionals. The Federal Reserve Bank of New York reports that in 2012, an estimated 44 percent of college graduates were underemployed. With the term underemployed meaning that these graduates took low paying jobs that did not require a college degree. Now we are faced with the question as to why these vibrant, educated college graduates would settle for less. Well, that question can be simply answered. CNN Money reports that in 2013 the average college debt after graduation was $35,200. While Thinkprogress.org reports that only 56 % of students who enter four-year colleges graduate within six years. Most students dropped out because of financial reasons. It is the prospect of debt that awaited most graduates, not the new beginning sold to them by the educational system.

This book will introduce you to the concept of Gift Economics and its potential to change your life's trajectory. By highlighting the corporate spirit and contrasting that with the human spirit, you will be able to make better choices. For illustrative purposes, a spirit is a supernatural personality known by the actions that it produces.

The writer is under no illusions that a corporate-driven economy will just go away. However, with gift economic thinking, the ills and inefficiencies associated with a corporate-driven economy can be minimized. This will also reduce the inequity that accompanies corporate centered thinking. Yet, as is the case with all movements, change starts with you. You can be the first one in your new community.

What is Gift Economics

Gift Economics is the way the humans were designed to operate. Contrary to many theories regarding Gift Economics, Gift Economics can coincide with the use of money. Money is not bad, it is the corporate spirit that attaches to money that causes a problem. Gift Economics is geared towards changing the current corporate driven economic structure in America. Gift Economics is the way that a majority of the people can change the tide of gross economic unfairness. It embraces many of the capitalistic principles taught in school, but rarely practiced in the United States. It recognizes an obligation to give, receive, and reciprocate.

Before we get into the transactional implications of Gift Economics, it must be reinforced that Gift Economics is a way of life. It is an economic mindset where the social contract with your community is more important than the currency used in the transaction. It is a way of conducting your financial transactions and living your economic life in constant recognition of the supremacy of human interests and common purpose. You must constantly place a premium on the supremacy of the human spirit over the corporate spirit.

As the title suggests, the term love captures an inspirational boldness that produces action. Love inspires, provokes, and produces action. Gift Economics requires that you conduct your affairs in a compassionate, equitable, patient, honorable, and truthful way because you are part of a larger universe which benefits from those qualities. Love gives you the courage to pursue your purpose in the face of the propaganda and rhetoric associated with the corporate spirit.

It is naive to believe that you can change the world by one transaction or impact the world given your limited resources. However, it is absolutely possible for you to both change your personal world and its priorities in a way that affects your bottom line and the world at-large. There is one thing for sure, you cannot keep doing things the same way and expect different results. After all, that literally defines insanity. Therefore, for most people, change is an essential element of Gift Economics. This change is to focus on human progression and your impact on that progression, and not money.

Gift Economics can contribute greatly to the US economy, but more importantly, it could be your essential investment in a future for the communities and generations to come. These actions embody the true American spirit.

Now that I have your attention, you may ask how you can operate under a Gift Economy, when the reality is that we live in a corporate-driven economy. A problem can be resolved by looking at the problem differently. In a Gift Economy, money may be a byproduct of commercial activity but it is not the focus. If money is not the focus then money will not be the motivating factor.

The essential element in a Gift Economy is the usefulness of the activity. A gift is not useful if it does not benefit the recipient of the gift. Another way to put it is that the gift must add to the value proposition of a person or institution. Activities or requirements that do not contribute to a value proposition are typically wasteful and driven by the pressures of a corporate-driven economy.

Yet, the question you must ask yourself is, can I imagine a world without money? If the answer to this question is no, here is an idea of what this world would look like.

In this world, people would still need to solve problems and come up with ways to improve lives. The only way that you could prosper in this society is to provide some necessary or useful service. This would require people to develop relationship skills and put a much needed end to the current trend of virtual relationships that have no qualitative component. Can you imagine communication that starts with a meaningful and thoughtful question of how the other person is doing, if only to see how you could be useful to that person?

This focus on usefulness would require the development of vocational skills. One person would fish. Another would build houses. Other people may train medical professionals or farmers. Economic life would continue. The development of these skills would be focused on real need and not on control of markets. Since only the real needs of humans are being considered, this would result in having some sense of the needs of the community. In fact, you would be preoccupied with finding a way to become useful to the community. Otherwise, you would not be able to provide for yourself. This is Gift Economic principles, and there would be no way out of this preoccupation such as welfare.

The more that people could use your product or service, the more choices you would have in your life. So then, your education would be focused on obtaining levels of understanding that would improve your usefulness to the community or employer. Your status in the Gift Economy would be dictated by how many people can find value in the goods and services you provide. That would be in contrast with the current US educational system, which is driven by an achievement-oriented structure that is disconnected from the economy and the community. There is nothing useful to society connected to a high score on a standardized test. The last I checked, there were no jobs available for test takers.

By way of example, when I coached a girls' basketball team, I was committed to making the girls better basketball players. This may have been motivated in some way by the relationships that were involved. Two of my daughters played on the team. The same inspiration that caused me to volunteer into coaching also inspired me to make a difference. This required me to study the game and to look for opportunities to improve their basketball techniques. One thing I noticed is that the girls that perfected jump shots were better equipped to play the game. I set out to figure out a way to improve the jump shots of my team. I began to think of a way to compel the girls to jump to get off a shot.

I consequently went on to design a product that would help with that. I received a patent for the idea and began selling the product. However, it is important to note that I was trying to improve my value proposition to the girls as basketball players, which is an essential element of gift economics. This also highlights how relationships play a part in innovation. People that have some emotional connection to their work perform better.

The obligation to receive in a Gift Economy is an investment in a new economic model. You can't be so preoccupied with giving that you do not allow someone else to be a blessing to you.

In Gift Economics, the social contract has greater meaning than the currency used in the transaction. This concept can stimulate a surge in entrepreneurial activity needed to improve the current economy and rebuild the disappearing middle class.

According to Mother Jones, Census data shows that the median middle class household income in 1989 was $51,681. In 2012 the median middle class household income was $51,017. These numbers are adjusted for inflation. The middle class is defined as those with income levels 50 percent above and below the median income. That is a meager $25,500 to a high of $76,500. Again, headed in the wrong direction. In fact, a recent survey found that only 30% of the people in the US believe the economy is headed in the right direction.

Each and every day people make choices on what they are going to invest in. What you invest in will grow. People cannot complain about inequity and not be open to receive from those who are trying to change the corporate-driven economy into more of a Gift Economy.

Therefore, those individuals, and institutions exercising gift economic principles, should be supported, as a way to change the economy. If a corporation, CEO, Investment Banker, or Stock/Bond Trader is making millions or billions of dollars, this money is coming from somewhere. More often than not it is costing you in your retirement if it has to do with stocks and bonds, as most pension funds are heavily invested in Wall Street. It is costing you in job opportunities for you or your neighbor if it is related to consumer goods. This is because of highly mechanized factories and poor quality choices where there is a lack of competition. When people make billions and millions with no increase in anyone's value proposition, by definition it is economic waste to the community. Not only are individuals being drained of resources by the corporate interests, so are government agencies.

Understanding your obligation to receive under gift economics would reconnect those community elements. To buck a trend would require contrary thinking in each area, which would include:

1. An obligation to support local individuals, families, businesses, and economies that provide useful services, even if it is at a premium

2. An obligation to not support the herd mentality that is the public education system and instead support alternative educational outlets that increases a student's level of understanding

3. Avoiding debt and developing ways to borrow from each other instead of institutions that charge interest, this can be through a community or family trust

4. Developing relationships within your community

5. Finding alternate sources of news and information

6. Developing nominating groups to pick politicians instead of allowing the corporate press to select them for you

This obligation should not be taken lightly. It comes with it a duty to inquire. This duty is to find out something about your choices. The corporations you deal with, the schools you send your kids to, the investments made on your behalf by your pension fund, and the debt related decisions you make. These are all areas that can be managed with a little effort. One way to improve the examination of institutions is to evaluate the function that they were designed to perform.

With respect to food, the farms and markets were created to provide food for consumption. This food adds to the value proposition of you and your family. However, when money drives the economics, you do not get what you need or what is useful, you get what the corporations want you to have. Let's examine your value proposition as a person receiving these foods and related services.

Your value system should demand that the foods be determined useful. Useful means that it provides the level of nutrition and quality that you need to survive. Today, most people compromise in this area. They settle for food choices that have not been demonstrated to positively contribute to that value proposition.

Genetically Modified Organisms have been shown to have undetermined health consequences as well as destructive environmental consequences. Yet, out of convenience, people contribute to that economic model each and every day. Yes, organic food is more expensive and inconvenient, so too are heart disease, diabetes, and cancer. The point is that the gift economic model has been corrupted when a company can show the arrogance to provide things that are not useful and consumers feel as though they have little say in the matter.

The obligation to receive can be realized by either the giver or the receiver. This can be done by generating economic activity in your own neighborhood. In millions of neighborhoods there are scores of fruit trees that produce fruit, which goes to waste. Offering to have a young person periodically come to your yard or community to pick this fruit would be an example of generating economic activity in your community for the giver. This fruit would be translated into economic benefits for the young person, and provide a useful maintenance function for you. Moreover, this may stimulate interest in the dying family farm industry and the interest of young people in food production, which benefits the community. Urban farming is the latest example where such an investment is shown to improve the economies in urban areas.

With respect to economies, families must review their wealth and potential to acquire wealth as a group. Family assets like land and property can be used to further the financial positions of individuals in the family. If families took inventory of their holdings, as a family, they would realize an increased potential to promote the wellbeing of the entire group. In many families there are houses, farmlands, and access to other assets. The foundation of this thinking is to have a meeting of likeminded family and an open discussion regarding assets and liabilities. This inventory would be beneficial for generations to come. This basic assessment is something that could start with the concept of Gift Economics. The corporate-driven communication systems have created an environment where discussion of financial matters among family is taboo. The fear being that someone may ask someone else for help. The key is not to deny the help, it is to support some useful activity in return.

The obligation to receive demands that people be more discriminating in their choices and their participation in the economy. Whenever we see examples of economic manipulation such as government-mandated insurance, where insurers are profit oriented companies making hundreds of millions of dollars, it should be clear that gift economics are not involved. So then, what would these gift economic principles be?

1. Companies that distribute salaries in an equitable way

2. Companies that contribute to the quality of individuals instead of buying all of the competition and then proffering substandard products or services

3. Companies that do not raise more money in the stock market than they could ever make in profits.

4. Individuals and Companies where most profits and employment remain in the community

5. Companies and individuals that you know consider and contribute to your value proposition in terms of quality

6. Companies that place the values of human interests over corporate interests

To reciprocate means to do (something) for or to someone who has done something similar for or to you. Today's economy is more about control than competition. In a Gift Economy, you must not be interested in taking more than you are willing to give. Taking is associated with the greed that has accounted for the current economic imbalances. Economic control is restrictive and debilitating in a societal context.

Under a system of control, some economic transactions are a big secret. Clearly no one could exercise the level of control over aspects of the economy without cooperation. This is true also for those wishing to change the economic system. You can support either a more restrictive model or a more liberating model.

Control is often accompanied by the manipulation of a number of things, including the truth. Students are not taught the truth about our money supply, the Federal Reserve, and why its meetings are kept a secret. They are not taught the truth about how the Petrodollar is keeping the money value stable because of the obligation of countries to conduct oil transactions in US Dollars. They are not taught the truth of how the top one percent makes money from the stock market, which benefits only them, and provides no value to society. In most cases that money comes from your retirement plan.

To reciprocate in Gift Economics means to provide Gift Economics for Gift Economics. It also means that lying, deception, greed and corruption are not allowed. Deception is associated with corporate-driven economics. Each and every financial action must be viewed through the lens of

Gift Economics. Gift Economics is bigger than just transactional rationalization. It has to do with deciding what you want the economic landscape to look like and then connecting your choices with that landscape. It is a cause that doesn't let economics escape the tests relating to contributions to humanity. Gift Economics is the only sustainable financial system.

To build an economic model there must be a marketplace. This market place forms the basic foundation for an economic system. In the United States the basic foundation of a marketplace can be Cities and Townships. City and Township Councils usually do not receive the kind of money that corrupts politicians.

A number of these entities have formed what they call sustainability groups. These groups are focused on the survival of the city, from an economic standpoint. As well they should, because many cities have recently filed for bankruptcy. Below is a list of those cities:

-- City of Detroit

-- City of San Bernardino, Calif.

-- Town of Mammoth Lakes, Calf. (Dismissed)

-- City of Stockton, Calif.

-- Jefferson County, Ala.

-- City of Harrisburg, Pa. (Dismissed)

-- City of Central Falls, R.I.

-- Boise County, Idaho (Dismissed)

Cities are the best government battlegrounds for the start of Gift Economics. Cities remain in charge of many of the land resources that are essential to human existence. Many also have an influence over water systems.

People need the natural resources of food, water, and shelter to survive.

For an illustration of how change is possible we can use the City of Stockton in California as an example. That city has a population over 291,000. Stockton has a sufficient population to start its own local economies. Stockton has enough farmers, builders, and a water supply to demand a restructuring of the economy. The city, if it adopted Gift Economics, would first compile an assessment of the needs of the people. This can be accomplished through its public works or community development department. It would then set out to determine how its community could provide those needs in a way that stimulates the economy.

The City could use funds from transit-oriented development to replace the redevelopment funds that were taken away in

California. Finally, the city has a port, transportation agency, and rental properties that generate revenue. Using the leverage of federal and local funds, the city could deliver the revenue it would take to develop the economy into one that is sustainable. This would require the elimination of the mindset that there must be big winners and big losers in the economy.

If you examine the use of the city funds, you would find that the city is spending millions on global corporations that it could keep invested into the community by way of its federally subsidized public works projects. Federal laws allow geographic preferences for local agencies where it is necessary that architectural and engineering agencies understand the local geography to satisfactorily implement a project.

It is extraordinary that a city facing bankruptcy, would not consider purpose oriented procurement practices to invest money in the city. These purpose oriented procurement practices would bring in state and local revenues and these revenues would contribute to an overall sustainability plan. One problem with local agencies in cities like Stockton is that there are too many of them.

Politicians should try and consolidate these agencies and their purpose oriented resources to change the communities. To say that federal rules prohibit the use of public works funds in this way is only an excuse. I happen to be a government procurement expert, and agency heads always pick who they want to secure project work. The federal government allows mentor-protégé arrangements for small and disadvantaged business. I have never seen a local government implement that program which could generate new jobs for the community. You would think a bankrupt city would consider this.   These resources would stimulate local business relationships, local social relationships, and local economies based on those interrelationships.   Corporate thinking is what caused the city to be bankrupt.   Its pension obligations were not in consideration of what is useful or the needs of the entire community. Gift Economic thinking could bring about the changes needed to sustain the city.

Some states allow requirements that employees live in a city to work in that city, like Chicago. This benefits the city of Chicago because workers have some emotional attachment to their work and their city.

California has a law, like many other states, which prohibits a city from requiring city residency, except in cases where there is a legitimate reason for employees to live within a certain proximity of the city. This was added to the state constitution by an initiative in 1974. A lot has changed since then. Over 30 percent of the city bankruptcies are in California. Politicians should have their staffs work on those reasons to use the exception, if it is useful to the local economy. They would not have to look too hard because justifications for local residency requirements are in city and state ordinances throughout the United States. In the case of Stockton, California, keeping the city solvent may be a legitimate reason.

However, city staffers are usually people, at the senior levels, that do not live in the city. That usually includes the city attorney. That is why certain decisions are made that do not benefit the community.

Cities merely need to plan, with the citizens in mind, using the tenants of Gift Economics to improve their local economies to make them sustainable. The more sustainable economies are not just based on dollars, but are based on relationships. Having people in the community providing useful services to others in the community must be the overriding principle for sustainable community efforts. Everyone in that model would be able to pay sales taxes, fees, and provide the revenue that keeps the cities operations going.

In this example, the people take money, relationships, and in some cases values away from the cities that pay their salaries. In a reciprocating model, the community (as defined by the boundaries of the city) would be focused on providing necessary services, receiving a value in return, and more importantly, perpetuating that economic model. The introduction of corporate thinking upsets the natural order of the community and quality exchanges among its citizens. Instead you have strangers to the community, primarily focused on taking, and not what they can give by way of community service. Community service is to only reason to have a city.

There are many gross inequities in the corporate-driven economy. Not only is the US workforce subject to gross pay inequities, its workforce is working longer, to the tune of 1,790 hours per year compared to Norwegians 1,420 and the French 1,479. This is well over a month's difference in time off of work. Even though they work fewer hours both countries have a higher median income than that of the US. This comparison shows that economics and economic policy play a key role in related quality of life issues.

As if there were not sufficient reasons to embrace Gift Economics, there is a more patriotic reason. Sociologists have studied the overthrow of governments and the people's tendencies for civil unrest. The Gini Index is used as such a measure.

This index measures the distribution of wealth in a Country. The Gini Index is a coefficient consisting of numbers ranging from zero to one. Zero represents perfect wealth distribution and one represent total wealth inequality, meaning I have everything and you have nothing.

According to the World Bank, the United States had a poorer record of wealth distribution than China in 2000. Stated another way, the Democratic society of the United States had a poorer income distribution system than Communist China in 2000. That may make sense since the US is purportedly a Democracy practicing Capitalism. However in 2010 China surpassed the US with a coefficient of .55 compared with that in the US of .45, according to a study at the University of Michigan. This is under Communist China's, Socialist Market Economy, dominated by State Owned resources. That makes no sense based on the rhetoric used by politicians and what is taught in US schools. The Socialist system in China produces more wealth inequality than the US Capitalistic System.

What that tells us is that these titles and the rhetoric that accompanies them mean little in today's economic world. What is real is that yesterday's educational system does not reflect today's real world. It seems that nostalgic terms such as Socialism and Communism are used as tools to confuse and spread fear rather than describe real world differences. The reality is that distribution of wealth in the United States is worse than that of Albania, South Korea, Turkey, Algeria, and Afghanistan.

The problem with the suppression of information is that it is hiding the obvious. Just like the "Emperors New Cloths", when we look behind the current economic system, we find a level of hypocrisy that should make us all uncomfortable. There is nothing patriotic about lying, cheating and stealing from the citizens. But what is more concerning is the reason for the suppression of information. The problem with concealing the truth is that when people find out they have been lied to, they get upset. According to the United Nations a coefficient above .4 indicates the likelihood of civil unrest. The US has a Gini coefficient above .4. In some ways this is a predictor for a change to Gift Economics.

In fact, I found out recently, through a survey of high school seniors, that schools in California do not even teach the giving principles prescribed in the State Constitution relating to public education and for that matter, that there is even a preamble to the state constitution. A preamble tells you why the document was created. It appears that this is not important. This is more indication that the truth about this country, its government, and its foundations are not important to the corporate-driven educational process in today's schools. In fact it appears that the educational process supports a model of colonization of the United States more so than equipping citizens to exercise democratic principles, especially from an economic standpoint. Colonization means to exploit an area for economic benefit.

Simply put, there is ample reason to distrust the current economic system. You must opt out every chance that you get of being treated like merchandise, and you must opt into efforts that support human interests and creates more choices and entrepreneurship.

What business schools will not teach you is that more than 40 percent of people with an Adjusted Gross Income of $250,000 or more have either a partnership or S Corporation. More than

72 percent of the really wealthy – people who earn more than $1 million per year – have a partnership or S-Corp. And nine-in-ten of the super wealthy – people with an Adjusted Gross Income in excess of $10 million – have one of these. What makes the S corporation different from a traditional corporation (C corp) is that profits and losses can pass through to your personal tax return. Consequently, the business is not taxed itself. Only the shareholders are taxed. This should be something that is taught in school if the goal is to equip students with the understanding necessary to succeed. Instead this information is treated like a well-kept secret.

Simply put, there should be more of an emphasis on entrepreneurship in the educational system than exists today. In a 2011 Gallup Poll, nearly 8 in 10 students (77%) in grades 5 through 12 say they want to be their own boss, 45% say they plan to start their own business, and 42% say they will invent something that changes the world. Although Gift Economics can be practiced in all areas of the economy, there is a special alignment between Gift Economics and entrepreneurship.

A report issued in 2014 by Babson and Baruch Colleges points to a trend in the U.S. economy: The percentage of adults involved in startups in 2012 hit 13%–a record high since Babson began tracking entrepreneurship rates in 1999. Many people are starting their own business because of the lack of equity in the current corporate driven economy.

Interestingly, according to Bloomberg 8 out of 10 new businesses fail. The reasons according to the article are:

1. One of the main reasons is that they are not really in touch with customers through deep dialogue.

2. No real differentiation in the market (lack of unique value propositions).

3. Failure to communicate value propositions in clear, concise and compelling fashion.

4. Leadership breakdown at the top (founder dysfunction).

5. Inability to nail a profitable business model with proven revenue streams.

All of these failure modes are addressed by the implementation of Gift Economics. In Gift Economics you don't waste your time trying to develop a business plan. You spend your time trying to become useful. An investment in yourself is never a waste. The US Small Business

Administration groups these issues in the category of poor planning. I would say that they are connected to selling something that people are not buying.

In contrast, defense contracting agencies, using the corporate economic model of control, employ thousands of individuals. Many do nothing but inflate the cost base so that profits could be calculated at a higher rate to reward those at the top. This upsets the balance and need of individuals to be useful.

This corporate thinking is exposed when one introduces the test of usefulness. There is nothing useful to humans who are more focused on a paycheck than the usefulness of their services. In a large corporate environment, many people feel dissatisfied with their jobs because they are not allowed an opportunity to be useful. These feelings are associated with the control orientation of many publically traded corporations. To these companies humans are numbers and not individuals.

For sure, you should not invest in one thing when you believe in another. If you believe in a more just, equitable, and stable economic future for the majority of people, then you must look at ways to contribute to that vision. Gift economic activity is a way to do that. It starts with your obligation to give and the establishment of like-minded economic communities.

How Does Gift Economics Differ from America's Current Economy

Gift Economics differ from the current US economy because it is oriented towards the progression of people and not the progression of corporate interests. Gift Economics makes a clear distinction between the two interests. This provides a different spirit and motivation highlighted by different priorities.

A person with a giving orientation sees certain economic opportunities as a way to help others. This can be present in the workplace and it can also serve as a catalyst for entrepreneurship. There are numerous opportunities for entrepreneurship, but many do not know where to start. To unleash this potential you must develop some connection with your community.

One way to look at the opportunities and exercise the principles of Gift Economics is to look at opportunities that present themselves every day. The need for high quality food, water or shelter; the need to reduce waste, the need to introduce efficiency, the need to improve relationships, the need to change product or process distribution, all represent opportunities that can benefit from gift economic thinking.

Today, many are confronted with barriers that are structured to separate them from opportunities to contribute. These money driven barriers can take on many forms. One form is the unnecessary requirement for a college degree. To indicate how arbitrary the degree requirement can be, some jobs merely require a degree. Any degree will do. You could have taken 20 years to get the degree, but somehow the degree signals a readiness for the workplace.

I was once employed by the Department of Defense performing quality assurance on weapon systems. I did not have a degree at the time. Despite this fact, I was promoted every year and obtained excellent reviews for my work. Today, this job requires a college degree. This is in spite of the fact that the job description and requirements have not changed. For this job, I simply took a basic aptitude test and received on-the-job training.

I then transitioned to working for an Aerospace firm. I was promoted again each year by this firm, eventually becoming a Major Subcontracts Administrator. My job was negotiating multimillion-dollar contracts for the company. This was in spite of the fact that I did not have a degree.

In retrospect, I was promoted year after year because I was one of the few hard working individuals in the company practicing Gift

Economics. I was preoccupied with finding ways to make myself more useful to the corporation. I would invest, on my own time, in ways of finding out more about the business.

My then supervisor, ultimately told me that I could not go into management without a degree. I went to school on Saturdays and finished my degree requirements. None of the college courses I completed covered personnel management. Nevertheless, after graduating I went into senior management.

During my career, and prior to obtaining my college degree, I had completed at least 40 on the job training courses. There was nothing that I learned in college that made me a better employee and more qualified to be a manager.

These arbitrary requirements occur every day in the corporate world and in government agencies. People must focus on changing this. This inefficiency is promoted by the educational lobby and motivated by money. There was nothing useful about requiring me to obtain a degree. Remember, one of the tenants of the Gift Economy is that the activities must be useful. If an economic activity cannot be justified as useful, then by definition it is considered corporate-driven waste.

Gift Economics is centered on the concept of giving. This is by no means a new concept, and it is extraordinary that human beings do not look at successes associated with giving as guidance for future behavior. America stands as the longest standing democracy for some very good reasons. One reason has to do with its solid foundational footing.

We can start with the spirit embodied in the Declaration of Independence, which makes the compelling argument for America to be free from the corporate control of Great Britain. Ironically, the Declaration of independence would be applicable to the situation confronted by Americans today, with Great Britain being replaced by multinational corporations. These corporations are re-colonizing the US and not necessarily respectful of individual rights.

To highlight the difference between a system developed under the principles of a Gift Economy and that of a corporate-driven economy, we can look at the educational system in California.

California spends about $8.00 per educational hour for the average public school student. However, students that are homeschooled outperform students in the public educational system. Homeschooled students graduate at a higher rate from college, earn higher grade point averages, and are better socialized than those who attend public schools. However,

California requires a teacher credential and a college degree to qualify as a teacher. There are no credential requirements for parents instructing homeschooled students.

The average class size for sixth graders in California is 25. This would mean that the public school classroom costs taxpayers $200 per hour to educate sixth graders. It appears as though the usefulness of the public education is not enhanced by the credential and degree requirements. It also appears as though $200 per classroom hour for sixth graders is high, given that parents and guardians are not paid for homeschooling. Home school parents and guardians could be paid $24 dollars per hour for just homeschooling 3 children at each home school.

This would pay homeschooler parents and guardians almost $500 per week for 4 hours of instruction to home school students. In this model, school facilities would be reserved for social and group activities.

In this simple analysis, the usefulness to the students and parents of the current public school system has much inefficiency, and do not further the students value proposition. This is true, ignoring the additional inefficiencies associated with the wrong-headed curriculum being offered to students. K-12th grade students today, study for tests that are not the best predictors of success in college or in life.

An orientation towards giving will allow you to stay connected with society. It will allow students to connect with a level of empathy needed to elevate humanity. A study and review of 72 studies of 14,000 college students between 1979 and 2009, presented at the Association for Psychological Science in Boston revealed that students are experiencing a huge drop in empathy.

Some attribute this lack of empathy to social media where people live virtual lives, disconnected in any quality way with their communities. Gift economics will change that orientation. You cannot give to someone when you don't know what he or she needs.

To become a chronic giver requires courage. You must accept that you are going against the grain and may be considered an outsider in many circles. However, as can be seen by the disappointing statistics of a corporate-driven economy, if you are not going against the grain you are headed in the wrong direction.

Millennials are the first generation in the US that will not do better financially than their parents. This is surprising considering the immense technological innovations that this generation has access to. With a world full of opportunity, this generation will still fall short. This is a clear demonstration that the US economy is headed in the wrong direction for the majority of people. However, if you are waiting to hear this reported on the corporate driven news, it will not happen. The news is not going to bite the hand that feeds it.

If humans are going to understand their circumstance they must start with the basics. The basic needs of humans are the need for food, water, shelter, and interaction. These are described as basic needs because without them, humans cannot survive. Survival is the basic building block for human progression. If you have food, water, shelter, and interaction, you can make it. Sounds simple enough, doesn't it?

There was a time when free access to these resources was available. However, as we know, in today's world, the majority of human beings are in the situation that they must rely on other human beings for food, water, and shelter. This would not necessarily be a problem if it were not for the greed and covetousness associated with corporate thinking.

When we combine reliance on others and a love of money, we move away from the basic needs of humans. Remember, human beings could not have survived without adequate food, water, and shelter. This was true before money was ever invented. To truly analyze the impact of money on the economy we must start with the fact that money was invented by people. Studying money as an invention will help you increase our understanding of the issues caused by money.

The first money invented was coins. Later came the invention of notes, which constituted promises to pay. Coins and precious metals were hard to manage and inconvenient for merchants to carry so man invented the banknote. These notes were as good as the person underwriting them.

Therefore, there was an element of trust associated in these banknotes. Ultimately, "In God We Trust" was adopted by the US to evoke a higher power than just any corruptible man that is underwriting the currency. Surely, "In Fred We Trust", would not be so compelling. However, it is important to note that money was invented to solve a problem. The question is, what problem was solved and what problems were created?

Logically, the problem solved is that money allowed people to acquire things that they did not have immediately available to them. Money became a proxy for goods and services exchanged by merchants. Supposedly, money was an instrument of deferred transactions. In reality, money is now used as the currency to separate people from freely provided resources. Today, it is the currency used to promote the reacquisition of things originally created and provided freely to humans which are food, water, shelter, and interaction.

Put another way, money provides a vehicle for corporations to possess a world that corporations did not create. Corporate ownership of a world they did not create, presents an unnatural psychology that is unhealthy for human beings. It also creates an environment where, based on arbitrary criteria, the economy produces winners and losers.

With the imposition of interest or usury, money ultimately became a commodity. Economy means the wealth and resources of a country or region, especially in terms of the production and consumption of goods and services. With the United States, we see the prominent role that charging interest plays in the economy.

Charging interest ushers in a new spiritual motivation. It is an unnatural motivation rooted in taking from humanity and not contributing to humanity. Jewish and Christian law strictly forbade charging usury (or interest) to a brother. Let us take a step back here, why does the Jewish and Christian World prohibit interest charges to a brother? What is so toxic about interest that it was included in the religious doctrine of the most practiced religion in the world? And for that matter, why did the biblical Jesus proclaim that the love of money was the root of all evil?

Like the essentials of food, water, shelter, and human interaction, money was finally established as a commodity. Unlike food, water, and shelter of which no person could claim to be the creator, money had no such connection with the natural order of humanity. It was not a basic need of humans, but somehow money became intertwined with their identity. People could claim ownership of money and thereby feel a sense of entitlement to all the benefits thereof. Money initially wasn't required to live, but now has become a social requirement. Over time, these two concepts blended with one another, as human access to free food, water, and shelter was systematically taken away by a collaboration of government and corporate interests. This increased the value of the money, which was underwritten by the might of governments, but controlled by corporate interests. Like all thefts, this theft has had some major consequences.

Every human is born with an enormous amount of potential. This potential has the ability to change the lives of other human beings in a way that brings about a sense of accomplishment and joy. This sense of accomplishment is in turn connected to some purpose driven activity.

By definition, people who have had things taken from them operate in a deficit condition. This deficit condition is caused by being perpetually confronted with the need for money. As we established, money is a commodity created and managed by corporations for their benefit. Becoming separated from resources provided freely in nature, and having to go through corporate interests to obtain those same natural resources has corrupted the natural order of humanity and frustrated the ability of humans to reach their full potential. Therefore, eliminating your focus on money is essential to increasing your human potential.

There is a way for us to take back what the construct of money has taken away from us. Gift Economics is the way to do that. Gift Economics is a way of conducting your economic affairs in a way that focuses solely on your physical and emotional health and the health of future generations.

Unless you were born rich, the need to acquire money has frustrated your development. If you were born rich, you may have become so preoccupied with money that you have experienced sorrows driven both by your preoccupation with, and reverence to money.

Since money was invented, it can be reinvented, with the average person on the short end of the benefits continuum.

Let's not be overwhelmed with this concept of reinventing money. Money is merely defined as a currency accepted by a government as legal tender. We also cannot downplay the burden that money places on people, through debt. It is the uncertainty of money, and the creation of debt, that has the potential to rob most people of their future and their future potential. Debt can be seen as a proxy for your time.

Gift Economics differ from the current corporate driven economic system because its transactions place a premium on your quality of life and the quality of the lives of others.

Economic Foundations of America

Some people believe that humans evolved and therefore, were created by nature. Others believe that a God created human beings. No one believes that man created himself. In searching for the US belief system established within the government, we find substantial evidence in the Declaration of Independence, the US Constitution, and all State Constitutions. These documents bear witness to the beliefs that support the freedoms and liberties granted to human beings. Those statements are being ignored by the US Courts and those elected officials that are intoxicated by the influence of money.

Every state constitution in the United States recognizes a Creator. Some call him God, some call him the Creator, but all recognize this concept.

Why is this concept so important? This concept is so important because the truth of a civilized world can only be guided by the answer to this question. Why did people create this great democracy? In essence, it is the mission statement for the entire nation. If people know why, then people would know how it was intended to run. That creates purpose. The ideals of American freedoms, justice, democracy, and civil rights are embodied in the explanation of why. We have the answer, in the constitutions of every state in the United States.

The United States of America was created because people were grateful to God or a Creator for their blessings and they wanted to create a country where those blessing could be perpetuated to the subsequent generations. That is the stated purpose of the United States.

65 | P a g e

More importantly, for our understanding, the things created were subordinated to the Creator. The subsequent governmental bodies that were created were then subordinated to the people. We call those elections. We now see that notion turned on its head by the concept of corporate personhood and the product or life blood of the corporate person, being money.

The Federal Reserve has a corporate personality. It wants to survive. Its creation prompts those invested in it to ensure its survival. The Federal Reserve has no interest in fairness, honesty, compassion, justice, empathy, or love. Those are human traits that will never be a primary concern of a profit oriented corporation. Yet, corporations make decisions that affect humans every day. Just as the loss of blood leads to disaster for human beings, the loss of money leads to disaster for most publically traded corporations and particularly the Federal Reserve.

So how do humans treasure blood? Humans have created blood banks so that they can have some available in reserve in case it is needed. Primarily though, humans are always concerned with avoiding risks or threats that could result in the loss of it. Human survival then, is a primal instinct instilled in all human beings. Most humans know, instinctively, that the loss of blood could lead to death.

You cannot serve two masters. Either you are driven by the furtherance of the spirit of humanity or by the corporate spirit. By its very definition, you can only have one economic master. So then, we see the tension between corporate existence and human existence. Which blood is more valuable? While the answer to this question was settled by the constitutions of every state, we see the courts and laws that increasingly do not recognize the supremacy of human over corporate life.

This is why many scholars say that money upsets the natural order of human and spiritual life. The survival of money has the ability to drive decisions that place its existence over the existence of humans. In fact, human consciousness and values represent a threat to the existence of money and its corporation, the Federal Reserve. This is why the practice of Gift Economics is so imperative to human progression.

It is not enough to merely state that money is just a tool. In this book we say that money is a byproduct of activity. We cannot, however, ignore that money is the life blood of corporations and the Federal Reserve. Corporate entities are focused on increasing shareholder wealth. Fundamental to that charge is a need survive and occupy space reserved for human beings. That is manifested in laws that subordinate human interests to corporate interests.

An example would be profit oriented prisons. It should not surprise anyone that money is paid to politicians and judges to put more people in prison. Most of these people are nonviolent drug offenders. Consequently, the US represents 5 percent of the world population but 25 percent of the world's prison population. To highlight the supremacy of corporate interests in this endeavor, McDonalds, BP, Walmart and many other firms, buy the services of the forced labor provided by these prisoners. How many human lives are ruined as they became merchandise to the corporations?

The most exaggerated influence of corporate interests over human interests in the US has to be Slavery and the Civil War. Slavery of human beings is the ultimate establishment of corporate interests over human interests. Those humans being Black Americans. America is still reeling from the demonization of Black Americans which allowed well-meaning Americans to tolerate this intolerable condition of corporate supremacy. The advertising campaign for slavery was one of the most insidious displays of inhumanity. This is why interactions between human beings must be encouraged and always elevated over corporate-driven transactions.

One way to make a distinction is that giving is the currency used in the Gift Economic model. It is the natural purpose for human beings. Taking is the model used by the Federal Reserve. The Federal Reserve utilizes the taking model because it knows that humans can survive without money. Therefore, they are opposed to giving humans the freedom of that choice. The US was progressing without a Federal Reserve, until 1907 when the banks held on to their money for fear that their latest Ponzi scheme was exposed. As is the case of their monetary musical chairs, when one bank will not honor its debts all the banks hold on to their assets for fear that they would be caught short. That negatively affected all of the economy.

Once again bankers had caused calamity in the US economy. In 1913, the Federal Reserve was created, allegedly, to provide more supervision of Banking in the US. At least that was the experiment.

What has resulted is too much corporate control and not enough human freedoms. Humans survived without money for thousands of years, in very sophisticated civilizations. People who are profiting from this current system will not voluntarily give it up, since it benefits mainly themselves.

While humans need food, water, shelter, and interaction to survive, the Federal Reserve is different. It needs you to use its money to survive. It needs you to feed into it. It needs you to support it. To the extent that it does not represent your views it needs to control dissenting opinions. This is done by controlling the educational system, the judicial system, news media, the government, and the stock market. This should be very alarming but not shocking to you. However, it perfectly explains our current economic situation.

One major casualty that we see in our everyday lives is the attack on the truth. As I mentioned earlier, our democracy in the US was founded on several truths. One was that humans had superiority over the entities they created. These entities are the government itself, corporations, and money. Another truth was that every individual had certain rights. When corporations occupy a seat above the government, as does the Federal Reserve, then that truth is no longer supreme.

Since corporations consist of people, it is those corporate mined people that give rise to the corporate spirit. That corporate spirit suggests that anything that increases shareholder wealth is acceptable to the corporation. Breaking the law would be risky to the corporation but changing the law is another matter.

We see in the media, corporations trying to justify that corporate spirit. We see most of the local news reporters laughing in the morning to pretend that all is fine with the world and specifically the US economy. We see the media suggesting that you will be happy if you could only get more money. This is a multi-billion dollar advertising campaign for the status quo. Money has become the crown jewel of human existence for many. People are led to believe that if they only had more money, they would be happy. Happiness is associated with taking and not giving. That is not the essence of human creation.

Gift Economic principles are American principles. That is why I started the non-profit, The American Gift Economy. This non-profit is focused on educating, acknowledging, highlighting, and making a distinction between the quantitative and qualitative potential of human economic interactions. This is done by increasing the level of understanding of like-minded individuals and the creation of gift economic communities, using the foundations of the US democracy as its basis.

The US stands as the longest standing free democracy because of its principles. Giving is the spirit embodied by the US constitutions. Taking is the spirit embodied by the Federal Reserve and its money driven corporations.

When people to go to war for the US they are taught that they are fighting for the freedoms and ideals represented by their nation. No one ever states that they are fighting for money or corporations. That is not patriotic and does not embrace the spirit of a common cause and a common level of humanity. It does not convey the hope embodied in our democratic principles. These latest wars and invasions are clearly more about preserving the dollar and US currency which is tied to oil more than anything else. Again, humans make sacrifices for corporate interests and its life's blood the dollar.

What the Supreme Court did was to elevate the corporate spirit by giving it rights comparable to the human spirit. The Supreme Court did not create the corporate spirit, it just validated it in law. Like any sprit, you give it life by letting it influence your decision making. In the US, we have done that. But the corporate spirit of taking is not good for human growth and development as is proven by biology and embraced by every major religion in the world.

Giving is a spirit that is far superior in the quality of human life and its ability to generate quality outcomes. That is the basis of the Gift Economy and why we all need to embrace its tenants.

This is such a profound sentiment that we find this foundational principle in every state constitution in the United States. In the preamble to the California Constitution it states, "We, the People of the State of California, grateful to Almighty God for our freedom, in order to secure and perpetuate its blessings, do establish this Constitution." Again, you find the same theme. In these documents you find a great desire to give and to perpetuate giving to others.

These democratic principles are rather straightforward. So what is the problem? The problem is that while many of those that established the US had at their core the establishment of democratic principles, others had at their core the establishment of corporate interests. This tension can be evidenced by the fact that men espousing the thoughts of a fair and equal world possessed slaves. This tension, contradiction, or hypocrisy is evident today in the institutions that we all depend on. The source of this hypocrisy was clearly money driven corporate interests. Slaves made money for the corporations. No democracy has a need for slavery. This is why the topic was not even addressed by those people writing about freedoms in the Declaration of Independence.

The Declaration of Independence states in relevant part that, "....We hold these truths to be self-evident, that all men are created equal, that they are endowed by their Creator with certain unalienable Rights, that among these are Life, Liberty and the pursuit of Happiness. — That to secure these rights, Governments are instituted among Men, deriving their just powers from the consent of the governed, — That whenever any Form of Government becomes destructive of these ends, it is the Right of the People to alter or to abolish it, and to institute new Government...." In this statement the people state that all men are created equal and they are given rights from a Creator. They go on to state that any government that will infringe upon these rights can be altered or abolished. Gift Economics would secure the supremacy of human rights over corporate rights.

Capitalism

True Capitalism is not a dirty word. Capitalism is defined as an economic and political system in which a country's trade and industry are controlled by private owners for profit, rather than by the state. However, a true capitalist does not need lobbyist, politicians, unfair advantages, kickbacks, or restrictive markets to flourish. Those are the corporate traits that treat humans as merchandise. The corporate driven economy has resulted in a decline in the quality of goods and services in most markets. That is because corporations focus on control and not capitalism.

Too much money in the hands of a few individuals results in corruption, greed, and inefficiency. Americans are creative, energetic, and capable. We must not allow the idea of true capitalism to intimidate us. However we cannot continue to let corporate interests ruin the democracy by purchasing the three branches of government. We must embrace a set of different ideals to change the wrongheaded direction of the current corporate driven US economy.

True capitalism does not consider a Wall Street or a Federal Reserve. Wall Street provides a forum to enable companies to buy the competition. It also allows people to make money without providing any useful services. It provides grotesque sums of money to enable public corporations to buy legislators and judges. Through lobbyist, corporations write the very legislation that regulates their activities. This is the Wall Street corporate spirit.

The Federal Reserve also affects capitalism by upsetting the balances of power that promote true competition. Legislative priorities in the US are set by fiscal policy. The Federal Reserve provides the life blood to corporations. Through its manipulation of the national currency, the Federal Reserve directs what is in the national interest. The US government stands guard over its interests dictated by the Federal Reserve and its money. Through its grossly fascist policies, the Federal Reserve is positioned to pick the winners and losers in the national economy. In fact, the Federal Reserve operates as a fourth branch of the US government without any democratic principles or ideals.

When the Federal Reserve dictated that oil will be traded in US dollars, oil became the commodity of choice for many nations. This provided incentives for oil based products and a disincentive of alternative fuel sources. This should not happen in a capitalistic society, based on supply and demand and the needs of the people. Innovation for alternative fuel products then takes a back seat to the need of the Federal Reserve to preserve the US dollar.

Supply and Demand are principles that work within a Gift Economy. Wasteful, money oriented policies do not. In a Gift Economy, opportunity is the opposite of control.

Corporate Personhood

Many of you are familiar with the concept of corporate personhood. Corporate personhood in the United States is a concept that has been embraced by the US Supreme Court. It states that a corporation has legal rights and responsibilities separate from the human beings that run it. This concept is currently the law in the United States.

By this action, the US Courts have given, from a legal standpoint, human characteristics to a non-human. In particular, the courts have granted free speech rights to corporate entities. While many disagree with the Supreme Court on this decision, we all live with the consequences of it. Corporations are allowed to give as much money as they want to candidates for public office. Therefore, the rights and interests of the people that work for the corporations have been subordinated to the corporations that they have supported and created. Subordinated, because the corporation has more money and influence than the individuals that own it. The corporation, which was created by individuals, may have values different than even those of the people that created it. Yet the corporation has legal standing in our democratic election system. In that regard the courts have given life to the corporation.

Corporations have a singlemindedness that departs from those of human beings. Corporations exist to increase shareholder wealth. Humans, then, become merchandise to the corporation in its profit oriented paradigm. Corporations will do what it takes to increase shareholder wealth. These soulless beings have been given civil rights by the US government. Rights reserved for human beings. Because of their access to wealth, corporations are better equipped to influence government and consequently the everyday lives of human beings. In this way, people have been put in a position to serve the very things that they have created.

Like the concept of corporate personhood, money has been given the same status and power because it is the currency of the corporations. It is what makes the corporations more powerful than the average individual. Corporations have the ability to raise enormous sums of money courtesy of Wall Street.

Monetary policy in the US is created in secrecy by a group of bankers. With the establishment of the Federal Reserve System, citizens in the US, are required to pay banks for the use of the Federal Reserve's money. In that way, money provides sustaining life for the corporate interests of the Federal Reserve. Monetary policies affect all of the humans in the US, but there are no democratic controls over monetary policies. Many believe, such as Congressman Ron Paul of Texas, that the Federal Reserve is unconstitutional and operates as a cartel. However, efforts by Congress and the Senate to even audit the Federal Reserve have fallen on deaf ears.

We know what the single-minded pursuit of corporations are, it is the increase shareholder wealth. What about the Federal Reserve? What does its value system look like? For the Federal Reserve, the goal is to protect money and its existence. This is the life blood of its existence. You do not need to be a constitutional scholar to know that the constitution gave congress the power to create money, and that the Federal Reserve is not a branch of government. Article 1 Section 8 of the constitution clearly gives the power to create money to Congress. Yet, this corporate entity, the

Federal Reserve, tells the US Treasury how much money to create and charges people for its use.

Just as corporate personhood creates rights for soulless corporations who have a single minded focus, personhood was created for the Federal Reserve. The Federal Reserve operates in secrecy and controls the US dollar. It is recognized as a legal entity, and is not a government, so by definition, it must be a corporation. Like other corporations, it exists to increase shareholder wealth. The shareholders being an exclusive group of bankers.

To illustrate waste motivated by a corporate-driven economy we merely need to analyze the US stock market, which has been managed like a Ponzi scheme of epic proportions. Let's look at the stock of the company Facebook. Facebook has a market capitalization of $216.98 Billion. In 2013, Facebook had net profits of $1.5 Billion. At this earnings rate it would take

Facebook 144 years to earn $216.98 Billion. Using Gift Economic principles, a company that needed $216.98 Billion to produce profits of $1.5 Billion would be considered an abject failure. In the corporate driven economy, this company is seen as a success. It is seen as a success because a few individuals and firms made enormous sums of money with the Initial Public Offering. The value proposition of the company, however, did not improve. The company was essentially the same before and after its Initial Public Offering of stock.

This scheme produces the waste and inequity associated with a corporate-driven economy. Through this scheme, gross inequity is produced in the US economy. In the US, 81 % of the stock market wealth is held by 10 % of the population. In a Gift Economy, no company would to be able to raise more money than could be rationalized by its earnings potential. Too much money drives out competition and produces inefficiency in an economic system. Companies don't compete, they just buy the competition.

What we see in this example is history repeating itself. John Law was a gambler that was born in 1671. He was one of the first in history to sell stock in a company. John Law sold people on buying stock in his French company, promising unlimited treasures as a result of their trips to French owned Louisiana. It was referred to at the time as the Mississippi Company. Law ultimately became part of the government and decreed that the stockholders could only sell their stock and not sell them back to the company.

If everyone is forced to keep participating in the stock, there is great incentive for those participating to market the stock so that they could sell it for a profit to another investor. Today, these people are called Market Makers. Later, Law mixed bank notes, stock, coins, and gold of which he had control, and it became a financial house of cards.

Economic models, such as Law's, that are based on control and not real economic activity are not sustainable. This is the case with Law, as his control created a financial bubble that burst. This is what happens when stocks, bonds, notes, or other financial instruments are disconnected from anything of real value. Ultimately, the stock value plummeted. Louisiana turned out to be oversold by Law, and there was a run on selling the stock. People wanted to trade the stock for gold but the government temporarily disallowed that. Ultimately, John Law was run out of the country when the bank could not honor the notes it issued. After that, John Law left France and went back to his life as a professional gambler, and ended up dying in poverty.

Ironically, the head of the largest bond company PIMCO was founded by Bill Gross, born in 1944, who like John Law was a professional gambler. Like John Law's model, people are encouraged to participate in the stock and bond market and the government creates stiff penalties for pulling their money out. It is called a qualified pension plan. The plans prohibit investors from directly benefiting from their investments. They call that double dipping. The government levies stiff penalties to prevent you from withdrawing funds from your retirement plan. Odds are that your retirement is making billionaires of some companies and individuals under the Facebook model cited above.

These corporate institutions are draining money from the very governments we rely on also. This is in the form of state debt. Of the top five states in the US, California leads the pack with $778 billion in state debt, mostly as a result of the state's $584 billion unfunded public pension liability. New York ($388 billion), Texas ($341 billion), Illinois ($321 billion), and Ohio ($321 billion). We should be under no illusion; the only entities that are making real money in this economy are large corporate interests. In total, American consumers owe $11.71 trillion in debt, an increase of 3.8% from last year; $881.8 billion in credit card debt; $8.13 trillion in mortgages; $1,126.0 billion in student loans, an increase of 9.6% from last year.

If government agencies and individuals are borrowing this much money, then it should raise the question of who really owns the money and how did they get it to loan it to the very governments they rely on for their existence? The answer to this question tells us who owns the government. Without the protection of the military and the police, such inequity would fall under its own weight. This phenomena upsets the natural order of governments and the democratic principles of the people who should own those governments. Instead, it is the bankers who call the shots and why governments are less responsive to the people and more responsive to corporate interests.

Humans are not merchandise. The corporate spirit is that he who has the money rules. The corporate structure rewards those officers who bring in the most money, even if it is at the expense of other workers in the corporation through layoffs and wage suppression. That is the dog eat dog nature of money based pursuits. Some intellectuals, such as Noam Chomsky, believe corporations are incompatible with a democracy. That their top down controls and intolerance of differing opinions, make corporations more like fascist's governments more so than democratic institutions.

The pursuit of money is the preoccupation of the people heavily vested in the corporate structure. Usually it is the people at the top. That spirit is what is so detrimental to the human spirit. That spirit is what has corrupted the major institutions that we all rely on. The mindless pursuit of money and the survival of corporations, erodes the quality of human existence. There is little consideration given to humans living a more quality and rewarding life. It is he that has the money has power and that power is something that must be retained at all cost.

The wealth centered corporate spirit is detrimental to human beings on many social levels. The fruits of that spirit are greed, lust, control and self-righteousness. When people do things primarily for money we all suffer.

We see this mentality at play with the concept of "too big to fail." Bank fraud and speculation ruined the US economy in 2008. Those bank thieves were rewarded by the US government on the backs of the taxpayers. Many of the bank executives were given bonuses the same year that the average person loss value in their homes and retirements because of their unethical deeds. Where corporate interests and the corporate spirit are so embedded in the success of the US economy, we are headed for disaster. These corporations are bailed out of their greed ridden predicaments on the backs of the taxpayers, forcing the democratic and human ideals of fairness and justice to take a back seat.

Current Economic State

The best way to understand the current US economy is to imagine that there was a small group of people that took all of the money from the majority of the people. This small group uses governments and policing militaries and other forces to make sure that people had to use their chosen currency.

To make sure that they maintained their advantage, they would buy politicians to make sure that the laws would preserve their status. The school systems would be configured to produce people that would not intellectually threaten their wealth by going against the grain.

In order to perpetuate this advantage, people would be allowed to go into debt so that they would not know how poor and deprived they actually were.

The media would produce a consolidated message to keep people from focusing on this theft, instead spreading fear, distrust, and entertainment to make sure that popular uprisings would get no coverage.

People would be taught to accept their position as merchandise to the corporations and that human interests were not as important as corporate interests. The following statistics provide evidence of this fact.

Underemployment Rates for College Graduates

Percent

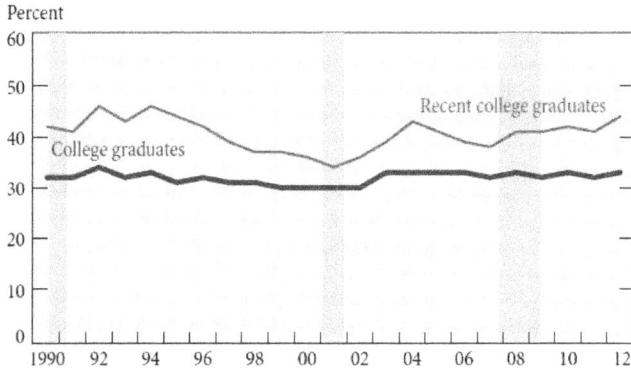

Sources: U.S. Census Bureau and U.S. Bureau of Labor Statistics, Current Population Survey, March Supplement; U.S. Department of Labor, O*NET.

Notes: *College graduates* are those aged 22 to 65 with a bachelor's degree or higher; *recent college graduates* are those aged 22 to 27 with a bachelor's degree or higher. All figures exclude those currently enrolled in school. Shaded areas indicate periods designated recessions by the National Bureau of Economic Research.

These statistical figures reflect the opportunity of our colleges and schools to do better in preparing our young people to provide useful services in our communities. The young people of this country should not be forced to settle.

The Huffington Post in 2014, reports on a recent Gallup Poll that revealed that only 14 percent of Americans—and only 11 percent of business leaders —strongly agree that graduates have the necessary skills and competencies to succeed in the workplace.

The facts associated with the corporate workplace are equally disappointing. Forbes reports that the average CEO makes 331 times as much as the average worker. The top 5 percent of Americans earn more money than the bottom 80 percent combined. According to Forbes, the combined income of the wealthiest 85 people in the world is more than the bottom 3.5 Billion people combined.

The share of national income going to the richest one percent

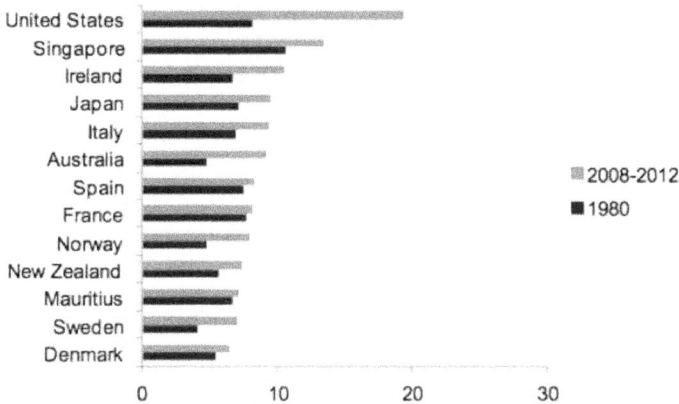

Source: F. Alvaredo, A. B. Atkinson, T. Piketty and E. Saez, (2013) 'The World Top Incomes Database',
http://topincomes.g-mond.parisschoolofeconomics.eu/ Only includes countries with data in 1980 and later than 2008.

Tables From Oxfam's 'Working For The Few' Report

The chart above shows how the percentage of the national income in the US is going to fewer people in comparison to the rest of the western world. This raises questions about the economic infrastructure of this country and the world. It seems there are several symptoms of a broken system, but no clear diagnosis. However, with closer examination the true cause of these symptoms is constrained economies, where the majority of the people do not maximize their opportunities for prosperity.

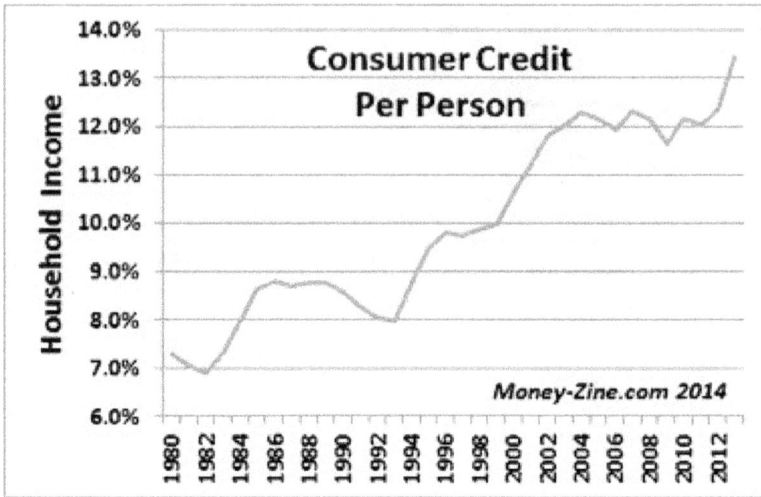

Consumer Credit Per Person

Money-Zine.com 2014

The above chart indicates that back in 1980, the consumer credit per person was $1,540, which was 7.3% of the average household income of $21,100. In 2013, consumer debt was $9,800 per person, which was 13.4% of the average household income of $72,600. This means debt increased 70% faster than income from 1980 through 2013.

If you owe people money, you are spending your time and energy working to satisfy your debt. Since you owe people your time, you have less time to pursue your potential. All of these constraints and limitations simply occur because of your debt. In this way you become merchandise to money brokers. This is why the media, education system, medical field, and their corporate backers sometimes treat people as merchandise rather than as human beings.

Although the incomes of the wealthy are volatile, they have grown much faster than the incomes of other groups

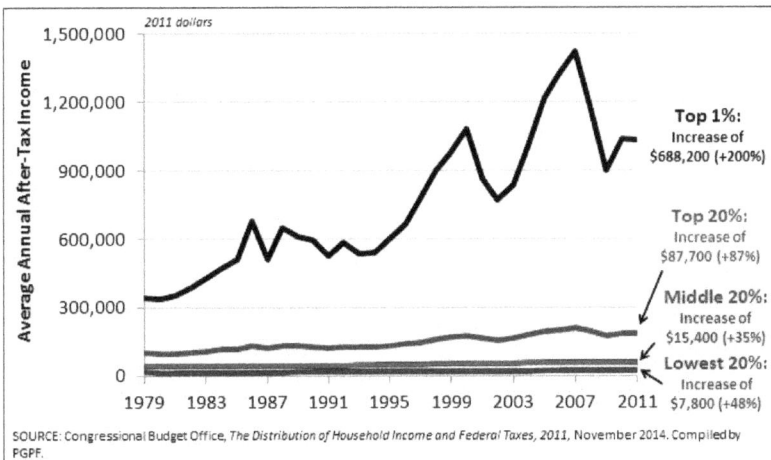

SOURCE: Congressional Budget Office, *The Distribution of Household Income and Federal Taxes, 2011*, November 2014. Compiled by PGPF.

The chart above shows that incomes in a corporate-driven economy accelerate for those who own the most money. This has no relationship to the usefulness of the services provided. This is more a function of control of markets and money and not contributions to humanity. Gift economics can only operate effectively when people operate to create usefulness.

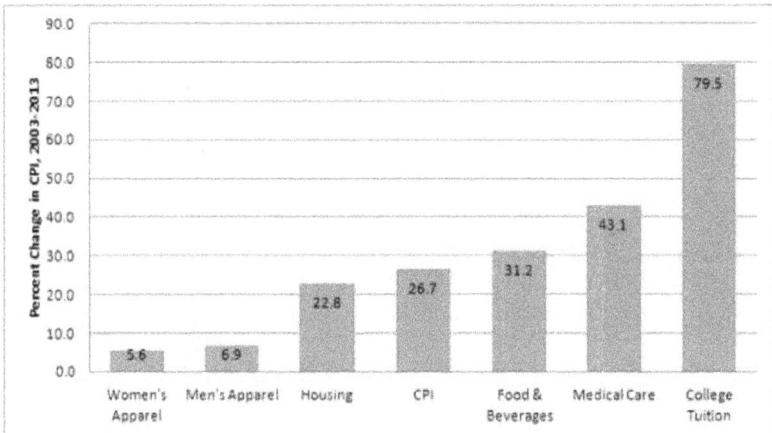

The overvaluation of college degrees has allowed the price of college tuition to outpace that of medical care. The rise in medical costs was considered a crisis and led to the passage of the Affordable Care Act. Yet, not a whisper about the outrageous burden that the cost of a college education is putting on our young people.

China has rapidly surpassed the rest of the world in the number of patent applications submitted

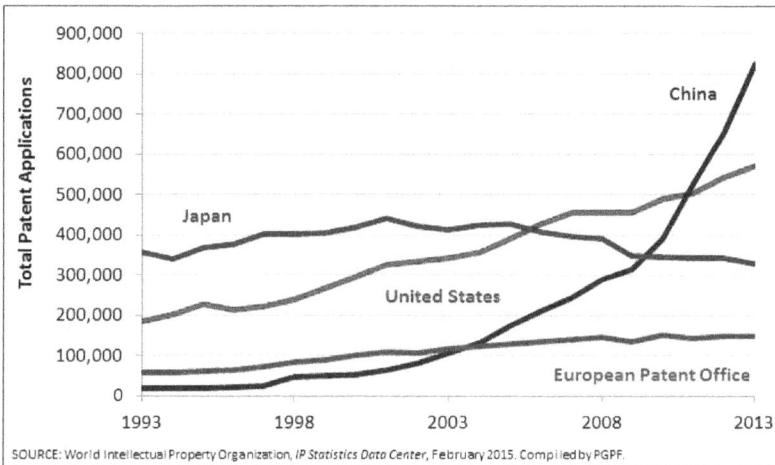

SOURCE: World Intellectual Property Organization, *IP Statistics Data Center*, February 2015. Compiled by PGPF.

Using gift economic principles may lead to more innovations and patent applications in the United States. Despite Communist China allegedly being an economy that emphasizes state ownership of capital, it has outpaced the US in numbers of patent applications. In the US it seems that the markets operate under more control than innovation than at any other time in history. Control is the opposite of growth. This is something that we should always remember.

Corporate thinking produces industry associations that create more and more hurdles to prevent other humans from entering into their communities. The legal profession as an example requires more foundational and continuing education than it ever has. This model is driven by the need of individuals to preserve their status in the economy. This corporate model is also supported by the banks who create more and more student loans. Finally, the educational corporations enjoy this model because it increases income for colleges and universities. However, Lawyers have been struggling for a while now, but it's gotten even worse: Half of lawyers are now starting at a salary of less than $62,000 a year, according to the National Association for Law Placement.

Not only that, but starting salaries have fallen 13% over the past six years, down from $72,000 in 2008. At the same time, lawyers' student debts are piling up. This is what happens when the students become merchandise. People forget that into the 1900's a college education was not required to be a lawyer. In many cases there was an apprenticeship requirement only.

Learning from the Civil Rights movement of the 60's, the press will make sure that economic rights issues get no exposure by the mainstream press and therefore not gain any momentum. Finally, people are being taught not to trust, communicate, or interact with each other because those invested in the current system realize that there is still power in numbers. But statistics do not lie. The amount of savings for people in the US has been on the decline for years, as shown in the chart below.

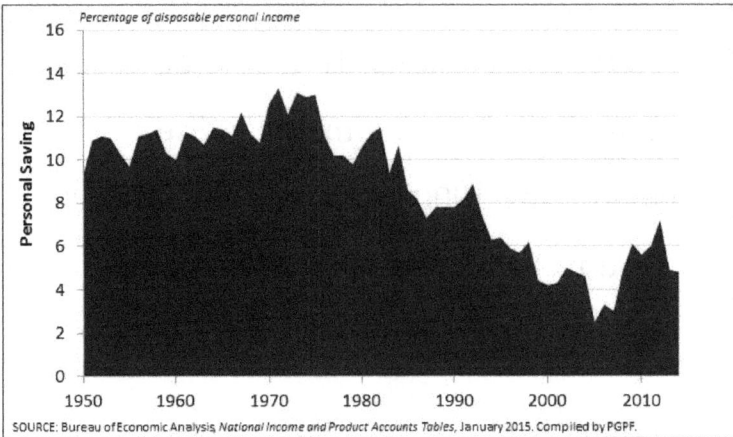

PETER G.
PETERSON
FOUNDATION
The U.S. personal saving rate has fallen sharply over the past 40 years and remains low at 4.8 percent

SOURCE: Bureau of Economic Analysis, *National Income and Product Accounts Tables*, January 2015. Compiled by PGPF.

©2015 Peter G. Peterson Foundation   PGPF.ORG

Along with personal savings being on the decline, there are more single member households than at any other time in US history. So the plan of the money driven corporations to isolate people from any type of community support is working.

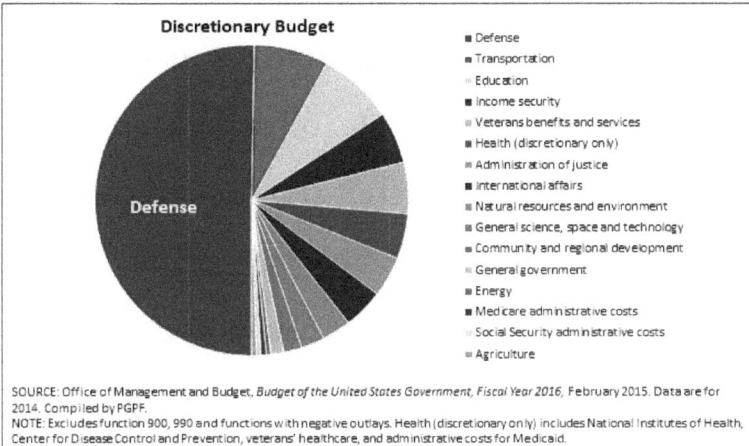

Discretionary spending funds a wide range of government programs

SOURCE: Office of Management and Budget, *Budget of the United States Government, Fiscal Year 2016*, February 2015. Data are for 2014. Compiled by PGPF.
NOTE: Excludes function 900, 990 and functions with negative outlays. Health (discretionary only) includes National Institutes of Health, Center for Disease Control and Prevention, veterans' healthcare, and administrative costs for Medicaid.

The chart above describes the discretionary spending of the US Government. We see a great share of the budget is spent on education. This is added to the $1.3 Trillion in college debt being added to the pot. You would be hard pressed to equate usefulness to the students with the amount of expenditures, which should be the test of the effectiveness of this investment.

I would be remiss in not pointing out that in the US, the public educational system, before it was hijacked by corporate driven interests, was focused primarily on furthering human development and on maintaining a useful and educated populous, capable of self-governance. There was a sense of patriotism not seen today. Vocational training was merely one of the seven pillars of a public education. This holistic view has been replaced with a narrowly tailored system, focused on meaningless goals.

To overcome the impact of the corporate-driven inefficiencies of the current educational system, students must be taught to separate the purely money driven courses and tests from the legitimate levels of understanding available. It should be clear that as long as the US remains a corporate-driven economy, there will be waste.

Parents must seek reforms that eliminate the waste from educational institutions. Colleges have a more solid reputation for promoting drug use (yes, alcohol is a drug) and reckless sex, than producing productive adults. Parents and students must go outside of the standardized public and private educational systems and secure opportunities for improvements in understanding.

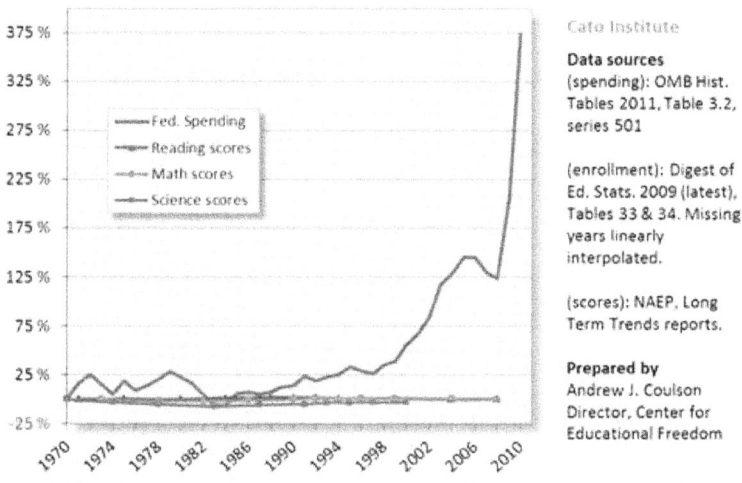

Figure 2. Inflation-Adjusted Federal K-12 Spending Per Pupil and Achievement of 17-Year-Olds, % Change since 1970

As the chart above shows, federal spending has not improved math, reading, or science scores in any meaningful way. Standardization goes against the progress of humanity and only serves to control and manage human development.

A more practical example of Gift Economics would be a learning environment where established professionals in many trades and skill areas would teach young people how to create things. The ability to create is the key to providing usefulness to others, and in a Gift Economy, students who can create are those who will thrive.

Still, the focus on usefulness cannot be limited to educational institutions. Government agencies must lead the way in not requiring degrees for jobs that do not require a college level education to perform adequately. Since government agencies consist of individuals, we, the people, have an opportunity to change this practice. It is ridiculous how the minimum requirements for government jobs have changed over time to require degrees. This has happened for corporations also.

Whites dedicate 47 percent of their monthly incomes to debt obligations. African-Americans needed to use 53 percent of their incomes for debt payments. Hispanics were the worst off in this category and spent 56 percent of their incomes on debt payments. In the corporate-driven economy the majority of people are languishing in debt. This should be a motivating factor in supporting and in receiving activities associated with Gift Economics. That would make you a part of the Gift Economic community. In essence, you will become someone who is facilitating a movement toward a more economically sustainable and just society.

Entrepreneurship Using Gift Economics

So you would now like to start a business based on Gift Economics but do not know how to get started. When thinking of how to get started, I am reminded of my childhood. Before I was taught to mistrust people. I went up and down my street asking people could I rake their leaves or cut their yard. It takes unlearning all of the mystery that the corporate interests have placed on the notion of entrepreneurship, and a very simple minded approach to starting a business. Just do it.

A good starting question is how I can help someone or some business by preparing myself to be useful?

This starts with the empowering assumption that you are created for some useful purpose. You do have skills and abilities. Everyone was created for a purpose. Everyone has the ability to contribute to the quality of another person's life. Everyone can be an entrepreneur.

You would then conduct an insightful evaluation of your natural skills and abilities. This would highlight those areas where you believe you have a gift or an advantage. Do not neglect things that you may take for granted. Talents such as having an excellent memory. Being able to relate to other people. Having a special eye for detail. Being able to conceptualize projects or outcomes. Unique physical talents or skills. Being a leader that people are actually willing to follow. You can determine these skills by your own self-evaluation based on interacting with others throughout your childhood or in adult life.

Additionally, you would evaluate the needs of the people and groups around you. This could come from human interactions, exploring, relationships, reading, and other inspirational sources.

This pursuit will require that you to explore and gain a measure of understanding in the chosen area of your pursuit. You need to learn how business works, remembering the tenants of Gift Economics. Some things are fundamental to business. The businesses value proposition. What is it worth to people? How or when do you collect money? What do other people do who are in the same profession? What is the potential for income in this area? What would you do different to add value to the business?

By way of example, I am a government contracting expert. I became one because I had an opportunity to work in this area and found that I was good at it. Utilizing the concept of Gift Economics, I focused on ways to add increased value to my clients. I then had an opportunity to engage in project management. I took this opportunity because I could see that a project manager was similar to a contract manager.

I then figured that I would add to the value proposition of my potential customers by offering to both generate their contracts and manage the contractors, as a project manager. This would give me a competitive edge in business. I was focused on providing the services and not the money.

A project manager has the responsibility of overseeing an entire project, in terms of quality, cost, and schedule. I had some technical background from being a Quality Assurance Specialist when I was younger. I also had government procurement background. I had never been a project manager, so I took a class in project management at a local college to get familiar with the terms.

I took on my first project which was a $14M public works project. During this project I focused on adding value by constantly investing in my level of understanding. The project was a success.

I could then offer my services as a technical person, contracts specialist and a project manager. I have done this successfully for 14 years. I can honestly say, that I do not know what certain clients are paying me until it is time to invoice. I never focus on the money because as long as I am being useful it will take care of itself. Clients have given me contracts and raises because they thought I deserved it, not because I asked for it.

This is what happens when you focus on knowing the business and providing useful services to businesses and individuals.

When considering market areas for you to explore, you should consider the basic human need areas. This limited list would include the area of food. Included in that category are health, nutrition, exercise, looks, and specifically hair. The area of water, exploring ways to preserve, conserve, purify, distribute, and sustain. The area of shelter, which includes homes, offices, repairs, landscapes, construction, sales, or household goods. The area of relationships, which would include education, media development, coaching, politics, religion, management, distribution, government, policing, transportation, preservation of nature, and sales.

You will need to overcome the corporate constraints to your thinking that will tell you that:

1. People are inherently bad and to be feared. Even though the number of murders in 2014 in the US is the same as in 1969 even though there are over

100 Million more people are in the US.
The murder rate has been declining
since the 1970's. Based on the data
from the CDC report, deaths due to
homicide accounted for less than 1%
of all U.S. deaths, with the odds of
being murdered in a given year at 1 in
18,989. On the other hand, heart
disease, the leading cause of death in
the U.S., accounted for 24% of all U.S.
deaths, with the odds of dying of heart
disease at 1 in 517.

2. Education only happens in the
   classroom.   Even though business
   leaders believe that college does not

prepare students for the workplace. Understanding happens through apprenticeships and real world experiences.

3. Failure is not a useful experience. Even though failure is the key component to the scientific method of discovery.

4. Distrust any and everything that you do not understand including different people groups. Even though there is no such thing as race from a biological standpoint.

5. Relationships are not that important. Even though relationships are the greatest predictor of financial success in business.

Corporate driven economics creates inefficiency because of its ability disregard the needs of humans and subordinate personal interests to corporate interests. Corporate control can limit the output of individuals that belong to its community. In that way, the corporate spirit can produce wasteful lives because in many corporate transactions, the productivity and wellbeing of individuals takes a back seat to the overall corporate interest.

Your challenge is not to become merchandise but rather to appreciate your potential by embracing the concept of Gift Economics in your life and fighting for Gift Economic Communities.

Gift Economics demands that people have an orientation towards an obligation to give, an obligation to receive, and an obligation to reciprocate. The object of this orientation is human development, not corporate development. These obligations constitute a forward-looking economic system. More importantly this orientation is psychologically empowering to each individual.

In doing so, you will find that Gift Economics produces a more successful economic life for all people, not just the chosen few.

Giving vs. Receiving

The giving orientation will bring the humanity back into your economic life. This economic approach is not just something that makes more sense from a humanitarian stand point. In fact, this orientation has been scientifically proven as beneficial. This positive orientation has not only been proven as beneficial by sociologists and psychologists, but also biologists.

The Proceedings of the National Academy of Sciences, a study also published in The Atlantic Magazine, concluded that meaning was healthier than happiness. Happiness was associated with getting, and meaning was associated with giving. The gene expressions of those that were happy resembled those of people under stress. This triggers activation of a stress-related gene pattern that has two features: an increase in the activity of pro-inflammatory genes and a decrease in the activity of genes involved in anti-viral responses.

The more beneficial gene expression is in people who have meaning that outpaced their feelings of happiness. Their gene expressions did not show the inflammatory reactions associated with chronic illness. Instead, their gene expressions anticipated more forward looking viral resistances associated with more social settings. This biological fact has also been confirmed in studies such as those documented in the book, The Blue Zones, which documents the keys to long life.

One of the keys to long life is purpose. So, based on the research, the essentials of gift economic thinking will help you live a more productive life, live longer, and make you feel better. Not a bad deal.

Relationships

Relationships come in many sizes and forms. What can be learned from the people that control the corporate- driven economy is that relationships are imperative to change the trajectory of the current economic situation. Positive and honest human relationships are key to evoking the change and creating the equity that is currently non-existent.

The threat of the prospect of unifying human relationships is why the corporate-driven press discourages relationships and effective communication, and instead participates in fear mongering. Does anyone really believe that it is a coincidence that all news stations cover essentially the same stories, in a consistently negative way?

Gift Economics demands the establishment of honest relationships. These relationships can be developed around common interests, common geography, or common ancestry. Most business is conducted based on relationships. Access to people who are decision makers is generally based on relationships. No matter how many rules and regulations are promulgated by government entities, the power of relationships will always prevail.

The number one factor in determining success and failure in business is relationships. Before the evolution of colleges and universities in the US, most professionals learned their craft from someone else through an apprenticeship.

Relationships with those who are going to teach you what you need to know about your business is important. In Gift Economics the obligation to teach someone and the obligation of someone to be taught should be very formal. It should be clearly established that someone is operating as a mentor and someone is operating as a protégé. This formalized process establishes expectations on that part of both parties. This current generation has an obligation to teach future generations how to conduct business. As mentioned earlier, only 14 percent of Americans—and only 11 percent of business leaders believe that colleges and universities are preparing students for success in business. This has to be overcome by vocational relationships.

In Gift Economics, the relationships with your communities are equally important. How will you know what you can do to be useful without having a relationship with the community? This community will be your potential customers.

Building relationships takes courage. It takes knowing that you have something valuable to provide. This knowledge allows you to interact confidently with other human beings. The fear of rejection has to be overcome by the need to be a part of something more significant than yourself.

It is corporate relationships that are constraining your opportunities. You must operate with the understanding that any group that does not work together will not survive. It is then, your duty and obligation to participate in Gift Economic Communities. These are communities where the social contract is more important than the currency used in the transaction.

Conclusion

Money can consolidate power in ways that constrain the natural order of human interaction. Corporations that exist merely to increase shareholder wealth, exhibit a spirit that merely considers humans as merchandise. That corporate spirit accompanies many financial transactions. Corporations use money to consolidate power in ways that upset human interactions with nature and spirituality. Corporations have the ability to spiritually influence all human decision making.

It takes courage to overcome the single mined, money driven, marketing campaign of its corporate owners. Money cannot be seen as a source of anything. Humans have elevated money to a commodity that serves as a protector of the individualistic, narcissistic, self-righteous spirit of its corporate owners. This is why the love of money is mentioned in religious texts. Which is why money must only be used as a product of activity and not the powerful idol that it has become in our society. Human interests must be emphasized over corporate interests in all cases. That starts with a love for yourself and your own ability to contribute to other people's lives in a positive way. This contribution has economic value.

To further appreciate the weaknesses of corporate-driven systems we merely need to examine them when they fail. One of the greatest failures in the US system, was the Great Depression. There are various economic theories surrounding the Great Depression. The Great Depression is cited as the worst financial crises in US history. There is the Keynesian economic theory that argued that the depression was caused by overinvestment coupled with under consumption. The monetarists believe that the Great Depression started as an ordinary recession that was exacerbated by mistakes in monetary policy. Marxists view the Great Depression as classism and a flaw in the Capitalistic model. The facts of this event are that, in 1932 stocks were worth only about 20 percent of their value in the summer of 1929. By 1933, nearly half of America's banks had failed, and unemployment was approaching 15 million people, or 30 percent of the workforce. The run on the banks was caused when depositors found out that bankers were gambling their deposits in the stock market. Whatever your theory on the cause of this Depression, corporate fraud and greed are major components.

Fast forward to the 2008 stock market crash. On September 16, 2008, failures of massive financial institutions in the United States, due primarily to the exposure of securities packaged as subprime loans, occurred. These securities were underwritten by credit default swaps issued to insure these loans. Exposure of these practices rapidly devolved into a global crisis resulting in a number of bank failures. The US Government bailed out these institutions using taxpayer dollars by issuing securities in the name of the United States. This time it was fairly clear what caused the financial crises, corporate fraud and greed.

These crashes were caused, like other financial crashes, by corporate-driven economics. Corporate-driven economics creates more and more people that get rich without providing any useful service to the people in the economy. With a monetary policy that produces a currency that is not backed by gold or silver but only economic activity, it is a matter of time before the bubble expands and the bubble bursts. The only way to turn this trend around is to focus on three principles essential for a stable economy.

The first principle seems so fundamental it is almost laughable. It is the concept of a sovereign United States of America. If you step back and examine the multiple trade agreements, tax policies, and immigration practices, the United States is being colonized by global corporations. Global corporations could care less about securing the US borders or the economic wellbeing of the cities, states or the nation. You see this clearly in the policies of the bought and paid for politicians. Now, if someone is willing to invest a sufficient amount of money in this nation you can gain citizenship. If you don't have the required amount of money, no problem, you can be classified as an undocumented worker. These are economic terms to describe democratic principles. You cannot manage a nation's economy without knowing what constitutes the nation. The ones that should be concerned are, "We the People." The good news is that the victims of this trend constitute a solid majority. Of the over 300,000 million people in the US, there is less than 1 million that are benefiting and heavily invested in the current corporate-driven frenzy called the US economy. This should mean that a solid majority of the population is interested in a change. This change is called Gift Economics.

The second principle is that acquiring wealth must be connected to some useful activity. Economic Bubbles and Stock Market crashes are associated with the ability of people to acquire wealth without providing any useful economic activity. When bank fees are not enough to satisfy the insatiable greed of banking officials there is an inclination to gamble other people's money for their benefit. It happened before the Great Depression. It happened before the stock market crash of 2008. Congress just included permission to do it again in the future with the FY 2014 spending bill. This guarantees that there will be another financial crash in the future. Ultimately bankers would like politicians to allow them to gamble with Social Security. Again, the good news is that a majority of the people are not vested in this model and therefore are situated to change it.

With crowdfunding platforms like Kickstarter, new trends in capitalization and funding are developing. In 2013, the crowdfunding industry grew to be over $5.1 billion worldwide. Crowdfunding is the practice of raising funds from two or more people over the internet towards a common Service, Project, Product, Investment, Cause, and Experience. These crowdfunding platforms must be expanded to include, more streamlined ways to support community projects. When the majority of the people are shut out of the economy they have the potential to change the economic model. With low cost applications and software programs, people are able to connect in ways that can spearhead meaningful change.

The final principle for a stable economy is the people must be conditioned to freely think for themselves. The issue is that the current US population has a herd mentality and is not taught how to think for themselves. In its extreme, this psychological mentality in known as Groupthink. According to Wikipedia, "Groupthink is a psychological phenomenon that occurs within a group of people, in which the desire for harmony or conformity in the group results in an irrational or dysfunctional decision-making outcome.

Group members try to minimize conflict and reach a consensus decision without critical evaluation of alternative viewpoints, by actively suppressing dissenting viewpoints, and by isolating themselves from outside influences.

Loyalty to the group requires individuals to avoid raising controversial issues or alternative solutions, and there is loss of individual creativity, uniqueness and independent thinking. The dysfunctional group dynamics of the "ingroup" produces an "illusion of invulnerability" (an inflated certainty that the right decision has been made). Thus the "ingroup" significantly overrates its own abilities in decision-making, and significantly underrates the abilities of its opponents (the "outgroup"). Furthermore groupthink can produce dehumanizing actions against the "outgroup"."

This completely explains the US mentality towards the poor, towards minorities, and towards those that do not look like us. This attitude is fed by the media and produces unhealthy, and dehumanizing outcomes. This allows people to view war like it was a video game. This explains the lack of empathy in millennials, more importantly, it explains why there are so many losers in a game that on an individual level, each person polled separately would like to win.

Just in case you need further incentive to embrace Gift Economics, I offer the US possession of Puerto Rico as an example. Young people are fleeing this area and leaving their families behind, because they have no economic hope. Investment bankers and corporate interests are buying up the country's assets like it is a flea market. The federal government is trying to enact legislation to allow Puerto Rico to file bankruptcy. Cuts in education, social services, and even food to prisoners are occurring. In the midst of this human crises, luxury homes and hotels are being built for the corporate elites. Puerto Rico is in a $24 billion funding hole.

What we cannot do is wait on someone else to change. We must become the centers of our own Gift Economy universe. This requires you to be courageous, informed, strategic, and most of all giving. This change will promote personal harmony, social equity, improved health, and a more purposeful life.

www.ingramcontent.com/pod-product-compliance
Lightning Source LLC
Chambersburg PA
CBHW072023040426

42447CB00009B/1708